Flight Path

Geoff Mead & Vera Grace Mead

Centre for Narrative Leadership

2018

First Printing: 2018

ISBN 978-0-244-43424-3

Centre for Narrative Leadership
9 Kingscote, Tetbury
Glos, GL8 8XZ

www.narrativeleadership com

To the memory of Raymond Geoffrey Mead

20 May 1925 - 9 November 1953

Contents

Contents

When Ray Mead died in a flying accident in 1953, he was 28 years old, his wife Vera was 32, I was not yet 4 and my sister Christina (Tina) was a baby of 14 months. His death had a profound effect on my early life and it wasn't until my mid-forties that I even began to come to terms with losing him. As a young mother, Vera somehow got on with looking after us. She remarried in 1960 to Harry Orridge and they made a new and happy life together in England and then Canada.

Even so, when it was time to bury her ashes, Christina and I placed her remains in Ray's grave in Whalebone Lane Cemetery, Essex. More than 50 years after his death, it was her wish to be re-united with her first love.

Neither Tina nor I have any memories of our father: she was too young and I closed the door to what memories I had soon after he died. But I know in my bones is that he welcomed us into the world and that he loved all three of us unreservedly. I am immensely proud to be the son of this fine man, whose untimely death was mourned by all who knew him.

Earlier this year, impelled perhaps by the recognition of my own mortality, I researched the circumstances surrounding his death. The scant information still held in RAF archives was supplemented by eye witness accounts in the record of his Inquest. From these sources I was able to identify the site of the accident and with the help of the staff and students of Kingham Hill School, traced the exact location of the impact in Kingham Woods. Visiting the site with men who had been schoolboys in 1953 and later with Tony Mead, Ray's younger brother, was moving and somehow settling.

Further research put me in contact with Mary Fox Linton, the widow of Ray's co-pilot Richard Anthony Fox Linton who also died in the crash. Both were experienced pilots and it is not known who was at the controls at the time. Mary Fox Linton and I have agreed the wording of a plaque that is to be placed near the point of impact, through the kind offices of Nanci Austin, Development Officer at Kingham Hill School.

RAF Meteor WL458 crashed here
9 November 1953

Sqn Ldr Richard Anthony Fox Linton
Flt Lt Raymond Geoffrey Mead

R.I.P.

*****

The accounts that follow are intended for private publication to friends, family members and interested parties.

*****

Oh! I have slipped the surly bonds of earth
And danced the skies on laughter-silvered wings

****

The bell on the alarm clock shrilled as the hour hand swept past 7.00 o'clock. "Turn that off will you darling?" said Vera. "I was up half the night with Tina."

"Teething?" asked Ray as he clicked the alarm off, rewound the clock and put it back on the bedside table. "I didn't hear a thing. Why didn't you wake me?"

"Because you need your beauty sleep more than I do," said Vera.

"That's undoubtedly true," said Ray, leaning over to kiss her on the forehead. "Seriously, though?"

"Because you're the one flying today," said Vera. "You need your rest. I can have a snooze later."

"But not now," said Ray as their son walked into the bedroom.

"Tina's crying," said Geoff in his best grown up voice.

"It's alright sweetheart, I'll go and see her," said Vera wrapping a dressing gown over her nightdress. "Goodness, it's chilly in this old house."

"I'll make us some tea and toast, shall I?" said Ray. "Since we're both up."

"Just a cup of tea, please," said Vera. "I'll make breakfast for me and the children once you've gone."

Ray went downstairs to the kitchen, raked the overnight embers in the range, tipped some nuggets of anthracite onto the fire and put the kettle on the hob. It would be at least 20 minutes before the kettle boiled; he went back upstairs, washed his face and hands and put on his pants, uniform trousers and vest. By the time he had finished, Vera was downstairs with Tina on her knee and Geoff sitting beside her at the table, still wearing pyjamas.

Ray spooned infant formula into a bottle, added a mixture of hot and cold water, shook the mixture and rolled a sterilised rubber teat onto the bottle. "That should keep her quiet for a bit," he said as Vera offered the teat to Tina's lips and she latched onto it. "Milk for you young man?" he asked Geoff, who nodded. Ray went to the larder and returned with half a bottle of Gold Top. He poured some into a mug and handed it to his son. "Cold and fresh, just how you like it," he said.

He returned the large, enamelled kettle to the hob to re-boil, made two mugs of tea for himself and Vera, and took the remaining hot water upstairs to shave with. He came back down in his RAF uniform, beret tucked inside his jacket. Vera handed him two pieces of buttered toast made into a marmalade sandwich, which he wolfed down.

"Got to go," he said. "Briefing 09.30."

"Are you sure that old bike of yours will get you there in time?" asked Vera.

"She's not let me down yet," said Ray. "Slow and steady does it."

He kissed Tina gently so as not to disturb her feed, tousled Geoff's hair and kissed Vera on the lips. "Bye darling, see you later."

Vera pulled him to her. "I love you. See you tonight. What do you fancy for supper?"

"I'll grab something in the mess," said Ray. "I might be late."

"OK," said Vera, "I'm taking Geoff and Tina to a birthday party this afternoon. I'll be back around 5.00 o'clock."

Ray paused at the kitchen door and looked at his family for a moment as he always did before leaving. Before they had the children he would leave with a joke: "The worst day of flying still beats the best day of real work," he'd say, or: "They actually pay me to do this. It's money for old rope." These days, he preferred just to look; to carry the image of them with him into the cockpit.

"Bye Daddy," said Geoff.

"Bye, Son," he replied, closing the door behind him.

Vera heard him kick start the ancient BSA Bantam motorcycle into life for the 40 mile journey from Red Lodge to the Central Flying School at Little Rissington. "I hope he's careful," Vera thought. "That old thing isn't very safe." Then she caught herself. "I suppose if he can fly Lancaster Bombers and Meteor Jets, he knows what he's doing. My worrying isn't going to help."

"Party this afternoon, Geoff," she said, removing the empty bottle from Tina's grasp and propping her up in her pram. "Egg and soldiers for breakfast and then we'll go for a walk, shall we? You can take your trike if you like."

"Yes please, Mummy."

The sound of the Bantam disappeared down the drive. Vera smiled and turned her mind toward the rest of her day.

*****

Ray stopped at the end of the drive, put his flying goggles on to protect his eyes, turned right onto the road and opened the throttle, leaning smoothly into the corners of the country lanes. The journey passed easily and Ray arrived at Little Rissington with 15 minutes to spare before the briefing. The corporal on the gate saluted as he opened the barrier.

"Morning, Sir. Nice day for it."

"Nice day indeed, Taffy," said Ray, recognising the guard who was a regular. He stopped the bike outside the Officers Mess, pulled off his goggles and glanced up. Clear blue skies. "Nice day, indeed," he said again, to himself. The mess orderly thrust a mug of coffee into his hand. He picked up his clipboard, checked his pigeonhole for messages, and saw a new poster on the notice board for a Fancy Dress ball on New Year's Eve. "Must tell Vee about that," he thought, downed the coffee and strode back out of the mess door, to a neighbouring Nissan hut for his 09.30 briefing.

Ray joined the 40 or 50 instructors, pilots and navigators sitting in rows of wooden chairs, facing a desk on a raised dais at the front of the room with a projection screen behind and several white boards marked up with plane registration numbers and allocated crew. Ray glanced down the board as he went to sit down in the front row.

11.30 9/11/53 WL458

Flt Lt R.G. Mead

F/O D.P. Wilkins

The WL series were all Meteors, but who was this Wilkins chap? He'd find out soon enough, he thought. The room came to attention as Wing Commander Ops entered, accompanied by his staffer and the duty Met Officer.

"Sit down, gentlemen," said the Wing Commander. "Squadron Leader Browne will lead the briefing today. Met report first, though."

Ray listened carefully and jotted notes on the pad on his clipboard. CAVOK (Ceiling and Visibility OK) – Light Northeasterly – SKC (Skies Clear). It was, as Taffy had pointed out at the gate, a perfect day for flying. Bit of luck, this late in the year.

Then the Squadron Leader went through the day's operations. At the end of the briefing, as the Airmen stood up to file out, he raised his voice above the chatter. "Mead, Wilkins stay behind, please." Ray had no idea what he wanted but walked over to find out. "Wingco wants a word," was all Browne would say.

Within two minutes, Ray found himself with a fair-haired young man at his side, standing in front of the Wing Commander. "Flight Lt. Mead, I've put you two together today so you can show Wilkins the ropes. He's done basic flying training and now he needs to get the hang of what it's like to fly jets."

"Get the hang, Sir?" asked Ray.

"You know the drill," said the Wing Commander. "I want to get him flying solo and qualified as soon as possible."

"Yes, Sir. How long have we got?"

"How long did it take you?"

"Couple of weeks, Sir."

"Well, you've got one." The Wing Commander turned to leave. "Enjoy yourselves, boys."

Both pilots stood momentarily to attention as he left the room, relaxing as he swept out the door. Ray stuck out his hand to introduce himself to his new charge. "Ray," he said. "Good to meet you."

"David," said his companion. "Likewise."

"What's the rush?" asked Ray.

"I expect it's because my father is an Air Vice Marshall. It tends to get the brass in bit of a tizzy. Look, I really don't want any special treatment."

"That's alright," said Ray with a grin. "There's no such thing as special treatment up there. What have you flown?"

"Mostly Varsities in basic. About 150 hours altogether."

"You'll find the Meteor a bit of a step up."

"The Meatbox. What's she like to fly?"

"She's fast and flies well within limits. Go beyond the envelope and she's pretty unforgiving," said Ray.

"Hence the nickname?"

"Hence the nickname. Don't worry, we'll fly her by the book. Speaking of which, get yourself a copy of the Meteor T.7 Pilot's Notes from stores. You can sit in the cockpit and spend an hour or so going through it. Find out what's what and where's where. Don't push or pull anything painted red. See you at 11.00 kitted up and ready to fly."

"Wilco," said David. "What will you be doing?"

"Catching up on bumph," said Ray. "

In truth, Ray was up-to-date with his paper work, but he'd wanted a way to change the subject. The Meteor's nickname was well earned and Wilkins had looked both scared and excited at the prospect of flying one. "Quite right, too," he said to himself, as his protégé left the room. He remembered what his own instructor had told him the first time they'd gone up in a Meatbox. "There are old pilots and there are bold pilots but there are no old, bold pilots. Not in this crate anyway."

Ray looked out of the window across the runway at a training flight of yellow-striped Meteors lined up outside their hangar. He'd have flown Lancasters over Germany if the war hadn't ended while he was still training in '45. Surviving a whole tour of duty was very unlikely in Bomber Command; they'd all known that. You gambled your life to save your country and he'd been quite willing to throw the dice, despite the odds. But it was one thing to get shot down doing your duty and quite another to fall out of the sky because someone had thought it would be a good idea to strap two jet engines onto an outdated airframe. But service life doesn't give you much choice, he thought. Ours is not to reason why...

He left the uncompleted phrase hanging and walked back to the mess for a second cup of coffee and a leisurely read of the newspaper before he made out the flight plan. When he finished, he went to the locker room, changed out of uniform into his flying boots and overalls and pulled on his parachute.

Wilkins was standing by the nose wheel of WL458 waiting for him with the ground crew.

"Visual first," Ray said, making his way slowly clockwise around the plane to check its condition. "Follow what I'm doing in the Pilot Notes."

He nodded at the senior Erk. "Anything I should know about?"

"Nothing out of the ordinary, skipper. Bit of wrinkling here and there and she's not got her full complement of rivets if you know what I mean, but all within limits. Checked her myself this morning."

Ray traced his progress around the aircraft with his hands, feeling the cool metal under his fingertips, checking for cracks and making sure the control surfaces were unobstructed. "What do you say, David?" he asked as they got back to where they had started.

"First time I've checked out a Meteor," Wilkins replied. "But I think she's alright."

"I agree. Let's saddle up, shall we?"

The senior Erk followed Ray up the retractable steps as he clambered into the rear cockpit and reached over to cinch his harness tight. "Full load, skipper," he said, handing over a signed chit. "50 minutes flight time, plus 10 minutes reserve, if you don't overcook it."

Wilkins climbed up into the front cockpit and strapped himself in.

"Cockpit checks," said Ray, systematically checking the instruments and controls in the rear cockpit. "Do yours by checklist, Richard."

Wilkins made his way steadily through the 38 items on the list. "All correct, skipper. But why no ejector seats?"

"Because Messrs Martin-Baker haven't found a way for us to bang out of a T.7 without getting diced by the cockpit frame," said Ray. "Besides, do you really want to fly this thing sitting on top of a live grenade?"

"I'll take my chances without," said Wilkins.

Ray signalled the Erk to fasten the canopy and to plug in the external leads of the ground starter battery. "I'm going to fire her up and get us airborne, David. You can get your hands on the controls once we get up there."

Soon both jet engines were idling at 3,500 r.p.m. Ray checked that the oil pressure and jet pipe temperatures were normal and that the engine fire warning lights had not come on. He signalled the Erk to remove the chocks and taxied gently to the end of the runway.

"Final checks for take-off," he called over the intercom above the sound of the engines. "Elevators and rudder neutral; H.P. Cocks on, L.P. Cocks on, L.P. Pumps on; Flaps 1/3 down; Pneumatics 450 lb/square inch; Air brakes closed; Canopy locked; Oxygen supply on; Harness tight and locked."

"Roger that, skipper," said Wilkins.

Ray waited for clearance from the control tower then checked the brakes were fully on and slid both throttles forward until the engines reached 12,000 r.p.m. The plane juddered and the scream of the exhaust was deafening as the twin Derwent jet turbines strained at the leash. He glanced down at his instruments for a final check, released the brakes and opened the throttles wide. The Meteor quickly gathered pace. At 90 knots, the nose wheel eased off the ground and the plane was airborne at 115 knots. It climbed steeply at 300 knots, until Ray throttled back at 30,000 feet to maintain level flight.

"What do you make of that, David?"

"Feels like I left my stomach on the ground, skipper. It's bloody quick!"

"At this height we can do up to 530 knots, about Mach 0.8." Ray dropped the nose of the Meteor and wound up the engines to full revs. The needle on the Mach meter wound its way round the clock. "You'll feel some buffeting," said Ray, as the Meteor shook under the forces of air compression. It was standard practice to test prospective jet pilots like this on their first flight – better not to waste more time, effort and money on chaps who couldn't hack it.

"Christ, this is fun," Wilkins said.

No problem there, thought Ray, throttling back.

"Time for you to get a feel, David. Keep her above 25,000 feet and below Mach 0.5. You have control. Don't do anything fancy."

Ray sat back glancing at the gauges every now and then and keeping an eye on the surrounding airspace. He knew how easy it could be to get carried away with a new toy. But Wilkins managed the unfamiliar controls well enough, completing a smooth circuit of North Oxfordshire.

"Excellent David, now we have to find out your single-engine critical speed," said Ray.

"Isn't that the same for everyone?" queried Wilkins.

"The manual says so," replied Ray. "But the manual is wrong. She's tricky to fly on one engine. Lots of asymmetric thrust so she'll yaw strongly away from the good engine. You have to correct with the rudder to fly straight, so it all depends on how long and how strong your legs are."

"What!"

"You'll see."

Ray took the Meteor back up to 30,000 feet, throttled back and powered down the port engine, and held the plane steady at 250 knots on the starboard rudder. "OK David, feel the weight on your right leg?"

Wilkins straightened his leg on the rudder bar.

"Now increase the power on the starboard engine to full revs and slowly raise the nose. You'll feel the rudder getting heavier and heavier as the plane slows down. Your single engine critical speed is the point at which you can no longer control the yaw and she starts to roll."

"Isn't that dangerous?" asked Wilkins

"It is if you don't know what speed it happens at," said Ray. "Try it."

Wilkins did as instructed. "This is hard work," he said as the Meteor's speed dropped below 180 knots."

"Lock your knee and brace yourself against the side of the cockpit if you have to," said Ray. "Standard Operating Procedure."

At 160 knots, the Meteor started to roll inverted toward the starboard engine. "I have control," said Ray, adding his weight to the rudder bar, dropping the nose of the Meteor and opening up the port engine to pick up speed. The controls became progressively lighter and the Meteor flew straight and true once more.

"So now you know," Ray said. "160 is about average. I'm not very tall so I fly with a piece of sorbo rubber behind my back to get me further forward in the seat and increase my reach. How tall are you?"

"5 foot 11," said Wilkins.

"Good, you won't need that then. Let's head back. That's probably enough for a first trip out. I'll take her in"

"Has she got any more little quirks that I should know about?" asked Wilkins.

"A few," said Ray. "The trick is not to run out of altitude, airspeed and ideas at the same time. One thing is never put your undercarriage down whilst you've still got the airbrakes out on final approach."

"Why ever not?"

"It does something whacky to the airflow over the wings. The undercarriage comes down one wheel at a time and if you get a yaw below 170 knots with the airbrakes out, the elevators stop working. Top Brass call it predictable aerodynamic instability. Pilots call it the 'phantom dive'– plane flips over and hits the deck. You don't walk away from that one."

"Do you think I'll ever get the hang of this beast?" asked Wilkins.

"Sure," said Ray. "You did well this morning."

He banked the Meteor to the left and dropped into a controlled descent to join the landing circuit at Little Rissington. Within 10 minutes, WL458 taxied to a halt by the hangar; the engines were stopped; the ground crew opened the canopy and both pilots had climbed out.

Ray gave a thumbs-up to the Erk to indicate that there hadn't been any problems and turned back to Wilkins. "Let's get some lunch, shall we? Steak and kidney on Mondays."

"I'm starving," said Wilkins. "Can we go back up this afternoon?"

"Sorry," said Ray as they walked toward the Officers Mess. "I'm scheduled for some asymmetric practice with Fox Linton at 14.00."

"What's involved in that?" asked Wilkins.

"Port engine shut down, single-engined circuits including overshoot and landing. How does that sound?"

"It sounds difficult," said Wilkins.

"If it was easy, anybody could do it," Ray grinned. "No fun in that."

Post War RAF Accident Record

Year	Aircraft W/O	Meteors W/O	Total Fatalities	Meteor Fatalities
1945	592	3	638	2
1946	1014	21	677	13
1947	420	19	176	5
1948	424	23	205	7
1949	438	36	244	13
1950	380	46	238	20
1951	490	89	280	59
1952	507	163	318	93
1953	483	144	333	83
1954	452	115	283	54
1955	305	66	182	44
1956	270	39	150	19
1957	233	30	139	17

*****

The Gloster Aircraft Company produced 3,947 Meteors between 1943 and 1955. A total of 890 were lost in RAF service, resulting in the deaths of 450 pilots. Contributory factors in the number of crashes were the poor brakes, failure of the landing gear, the high fuel consumption and consequent short flight endurance causing pilots to run out of fuel, and difficult handling with one engine out due to the widely set engines.

RAF Records

Wing Commander Roland Beaumont, Chief Test Pilot English Electric Aviation, said of his first flight in a Gloster Meteor, 1944. *It ought to have been an impressive experience, but somehow it was not... the stiffening controls confirmed that we were not only going fast but that we had no operational maneuverability worth mentioning.*

*****

Extract from RAF Records

09-11-53, Gloster Meteor T.7, WL458, Kingham, Oxfordshire. *Whilst carrying out an asymmetric sortie, the aircraft became inverted and struck trees,* Sq Ldr Richard Anthony Fox-Linton, Flt Lt Raymond Geoffrey Mead both died in the accident.

RAF Accident Card – Meteor T7 WL 458

A/C in an inverted attitude of about 60 degrees to the ground struck tall trees and subsequently the ground, the engines were under power on impact, u/c locked down, flaps in and dive brakes closed.

Pilots were engaged on a mutual asymmetric exercise. It is thought that from the time the A/C had been airborne and the fact that the u/c was down they were carrying out practice asymmetric circuits at height. The facts established from the examination of the wreckage, A/C rolling with engines under power, points to the probability that critical speed had been exceeded with consequent loss of control at low altitude.

Statement taken by Constable 61 Coxon on 10 November 1953 from John Arthur Lee, Manor Cottage, Kingham, Oxon. Agricultural worker, aged 30.

Soon after 2 pm on Monday the 9th November I saw a Meteor plane flying across Kingham at about 3 to 400 feet, the plane had its two main wheels down, I was unable to se the nose wheel. The plane was flying with the nose well up.

My attention was drawn to the plane by a sound which was similar to a re-heat being operated, there was no smoke or signs of any debris falling. The plane then seemed to drop each wing in turn and just fell out of the sky, at this time I could not say if the wheels were down or not.

The engines remained on the whole time

Statement taken by Constable 61 Coxon on 10 November 1953 from William Alldiss, Erdington House, Kingham, Oxon. Retired Engineer, aged 70.

Shortly after 2 pm on Monday the 9th November I was in my garden when a very loud explosion drew my attention to a jet aircraft flying overhead. There was no smoke or pieces falling from the plane.

The plane then did several rolls and disappeared beyond the trees.

The speed seemed slow for a jet plane and it was flying low and I realised it was too low to recover.

The plane rolled right handed before the crash.

Statement taken by Constable 61 Coxon on 10 November 1953 from Albert William Plowman, Kingham Hill, Kingham, Oxon. Tractor Driver, aged 37.

On Monday afternoon the 9th November I was working in Stratford Wood, at some time after 2 pm I noticed an aircraft coming from the direction of Rissington.

Looking up through the trees I saw the plane was very low and rolling to the left, the tail was down and the nose was up. There did not appear to be a great deal of noise, the plane straightened out, dipped forward then rose a little before finally dropping a wing and diving into the ground about 70 yards away. There was a muffled explosion and a flash as it hit.

Statement taken by Constable 61 Coxon on 10 November 1953 from Geoffrey Hart Phelps, Sheffield House, Kingham Hill. Housemaster, aged 53.

At about 2.15 pm on Monday the 9th November I heard the sound of jet engines and looking up I saw the plane approaching from the direction of Little Rissington.

The plane was unusually low and the engines seemed full on the whole time. It seemed to roll in one direction, checked and rolled the other way, The final rolls were right handed.

The wheels were definitely in the up position when I saw the plane and I heard no explosion prior to the crash.

Report of Constable 61 Coxon, Churchill Police Station, Oxfordshire
Constabulary, dated 9 November 1953.

<u>Aircraft crash at Kingham 9.11.53.</u>

At approximately 1420 hours on Monday the 9th November
1953, I received information from Sub/Div Station to the effect that
an aircraft had been reported crashing near Kingham Hill.

I was almost immediately picked up [by Sgt. McDermott]
and went to the scene of the crash, which was indicated by a plume
of grey smoke and further marked by other aircraft orbiting.

The aircraft, a two-seat Meteor trainer, had crashed at point
(Map ref. 273256) in a small wood among the dispersed buildings of
Kingham Hill School.

On arrival at approx. 1430 hours the wreckage was spread
over a considerable area and still burning but not fiercely. The two
occupants were obviously killed outright and the two charred bodies were in the centre of the smouldering wreckage.

The Chipping Norton Fire Service arrived shortly afterwards together with the Ambulance, the former extinguishing the
small fires. The bodies were covered with asbestos blankets.... Some
six or seven trees were destroyed and others damaged, no other
property was affected.

Statements will be obtained from the several eye witnesses
in due course and submitted.

The sun hangs low in the clear blue sky of a halcyon winter afternoon. At 1,500 feet, the ground is close enough for you to name the clusters of farm buildings and distinguish the individual trees dotting the hedgerows that separate fields and pastures. It's a familiar landscape; a single glance is sufficient to judge your direction of travel and position relative to Little Rissington.

Your torso, clamped into the contours of the bucket seat by the harness, aches from excessive G-Force and your legs tremble from the pressure you have to exert on the rudder bar, when flying asymmetric. You push the regular banshee howl of the jet to the back of your mind so you can hear the engine note changing in response to the controls: the rising pitch of the crescendo as you push the throttle forward and wait for the turbine to spool up; the diminuendo when you ease back to decelerate. The ever-present whiff of aviation fuel creeps through the seal of your oxygen mask and assails your nostrils. The sour taste of bile burns at the back of your throat. Your eyes constantly flick between the gauges inside the cockpit and the surrounding airspace, checking, checking, checking.

There's enough fuel for another circuit. Port engine shut down; hard right rudder to counteract the yaw; slow to 170 knots; air brakes in, undercarriage down and locked; simulated landing at a 'hard deck' of 1,000 feet.

Perfect.

Power up starboard engine, pull up. Climb. Climb.

But the Meteor doesn't climb. Instead it begins to slip sideways as the thrust of the starboard engine overpowers your frantic efforts to hold full right rudder. The port wing loses lift and the plane starts to crab across the sky. A huge hit of adrenaline kicks your brain into overdrive, instantly making the world drop into slow motion.

You're approaching Kingham Hill. The school buildings are coming up fast. You are already too low to get more speed by dropping the nose and the more throttle you apply to the remaining engine, the greater the yaw. There's no time to restart the port engine and no way to gain altitude. On this flight path you calculate that you will plough into the main hall. Your options are vanishing moment by moment. You are going to crash. The only choice you have is whether to crash sooner or later. Later will give you a few more seconds of life. Sooner might just save the school.

This is how it happens, you think – the sudden rent in the fabric between the worlds that allows fate to claim you without warning. You are surprised at just how calm you feel. You think of your wife and family, of the years you might have had, of children yet unborn; you think of your friends and those who have gone before. Mostly, you feel gratitude for the joy you have had in the life you are about to lose. A smile plays about your lips.

Deliberately, you unlock your right knee and release the rudder bar. The yaw increases, the plane rolls, inverts and drops like a stone toward the plantation of bare trees that stands between you and the school.

Your adrenaline-fuelled brain and slow motion vision have done their work. There's nothing to do now except look out of the cockpit. The sky seems to turn brown, as you fall upside-down into the wood. The plane smashes through the tree trunks and disintegrates as it hits the ground.

Brown turns instantly to black and then, for a timeless moment, to a brilliant white light which you decide to follow.

Boys run pell-mell from the school into the wood to see the remains.

A silent music hangs in the air.

They will remember it for the rest of their lives.

*****

I remember the crash very clearly and that it happened in the afternoon. At that time I would have been nearly 11 years old and in Plymouth House where about 30 junior boys lived. This house was below the pine plantation where your father's plane came down and we had to walk up to the main school each day through the plantation. The crash site was more or less in the middle of the plantation and about 50 yards in from the road. I can remember the RAF recovery team were camped on the edge of the road for a number of days and we passed by them twice a day on our way to and from school. Eventually, a low loader arrived and removed the remains of the aircraft. After the RAF left, we were free to go back into the plantation and of course visit the crash site where there was still an amount of debris. I recollect that only a few trees had been damaged, indicating that the aircraft had not crashed after a gliding impact. I cannot remember there being any evidence that there had been a fire on impact but do remember a small crater that must have been made by the nose of the Meteor.

Alastair Ball, pupil at KHS

I was at KHS in 1953, I was 15 at the time, and saw the plane crash. I was asked to give a statement to somebody, from what I believe is now known as the AIB, telling them what I saw. At the time I remember saying that the plane was diving at about 30°, a guess that I later amended with these words being added to my statement, "I think the angle may not have been as much as thirty degrees."

Although it was 65 years ago I can still see the plane coming down. I was viewing the plane from its port side; it was travelling at a slow speed for a jet aircraft, which I would now interpret as being unable to generate sufficient lift to clear the hill. Its direction of flight would have been a few degrees either side of due north, which would have put the refectory and then the main school building, directly in its path. I remember that, at that shallow angle, which I now believe was about 15°; it would probably have hit one or both of the aforementioned buildings. At the point where it was barely above the treetops it suddenly dipped down and crashed into the trees.

I didn't see the aircraft immediately after the crash, but I did see it on the following day. At that time its remains were upright with the nose pointing towards the school buildings. It is my belief that the brave, selfless pilot[s] deliberately crashed into the trees to avoid hitting the school buildings.

Tony "Jock" Norton, pupil at KHS

I was in the Kingham Hill School Library at the time. We were used to planes due to the proximity of Little Rissington, however this Meteor grabbed my attention as it was unusually low and loud. Looking through the windows, which faced East, it seemed to be circling. Then I lost sight of it. I don't remember hearing a crash but I did go down to the crash site eventually that day. This was in the plantation to the West side of the road leading down to Plymouth House Hostel and just below the Chaplain's House. The smell of jet fuel was overpowering.

Richard Huckle, pupil at KHS.

I remember hearing the screeching of the plane overhead as it passed over the school but nothing immediately after the accident. I was 11 at the time and being in Plymouth House we had to attend lessons at the Main School passing through the centre of the plantation. Being in winter, it was quite dark when we walked back to Plymouth House and we used to stop and talk to the RAF officers that were guarding the crash site. The crash took place very close to the road that led from the main school to Sarsden Halt.

John Shearer, pupil at KHS

****

This is where you died all those years ago,
among the wreckage and the burning trees.
Your death, which came so long before its time,
bestowed a kind of immortality.

Forever young and handsome in our minds,
your short life unscarred by disappointment,
nor yet embittered by the passing years.
How could we do anything but love you?

We made you into what we wanted most:
the perfect father, husband, brother, son
because the fantasies were all we had
to fill the yearning emptiness of grief.

Now I am older than you ever were,
I meet you face-to-face and find myself
ashamed that I have failed to do enough
though still I hope you would be proud of me.

For that's the dearest wish of every son,
his father's benediction and his love.
I listen to the birdsong in the woods
and hear your voice, anointing me with grace.

*****

Ray was posted to RAF Little Rissington when er came back from Malta. We started off in a part of a house in Cirencester until he found something a bit nearer. We then moved to Red Lodge, Purton, Wiltshire. It was a huge house and when there had been money to spend on it, it must have been lovely. I never managed to finish counting the number of rooms. We had what in fact had been the servants' quarters. Adjustments had been made and the owners had for a long time been taking in officers' families, for many years in fact. We had three bedrooms, a sitting-room and bathroom upstairs and a huge kitchen and walk-in larder room and an enormous dining room, which always seemed to be freezing, downstairs.

The grounds were a delight. Two drives leading out east and west, both at least a mile long. So to take Geoff and Tina for a walk meant that I didn't have to leave the grounds. Geoff had a tiny three-wheeled bike and I would push Tina's big pram. I recall the weather being very good. I think we must have moved there sometime in July. There were fields beside these long drives and one had a couple of cows in. They were so tame that they would follow along by the fence beside us as far as we walked and back again when we turned to go home. This was a good fun thing for Geoff who liked to backpedal sometimes to see if they would follow him.

The grounds were great for the children and we had free run of everywhere outside. The gardens were taken good care of mainly by the daughter of the house. One weekend Ray and I and the youngsters were out walking and Ray said: "No question about what this lad needs for Christmas – a new bike, this thing is far too small for him!"

In late October 1953 we were invited to a cocktail party given in the house where we lived by the owners Mr. and Mrs. Ward. They knew all the local folks of course including the dentist and his wife who had two small children. She and I got chatting and she said that one of her youngsters had a birthday party coming up and why not take Geoff and Tina over.

Her husband came and picked us up after just lunch [on 9th November] and drove us back to the Red Lodge about 5.00pm. It was a Monday, Geoff and Tina had had their bath and were more or less ready for bed when a voice from downstairs called me, saying there was a phone call for me.

It was in fact Ray's Aunt whom we had already invited to visit and at first I thought she was just phoning to say she was coming so that was how I greeted her. She instantly went silent and I said: "Are you still there?" thinking she had been cut off. Her next words will stick in my memory for all time.

"You don't know, do you?"

She then told me that the police had been, going first to Tony's house (Ray's younger brother) and had told them that Ray had been killed. She had had to go to a phone box to make the call. I learned afterwards, that she went back home feeling that it was all a mistake, as I knew nothing about it.

I can't really say how I felt. I expect I was in total shock. I didn't burst into tears, just completely numb. I told Mrs. Ward as she passed me coming out from the telephone and she phoned RAF Little Rissington and they confirmed it and said that the Commandant was on his way to me. He and his wife arrived very shortly afterwards. I seemed to be behaving like a zombie. I had put Geoff and Tina to bed before they came.

There were so many things that were not told to me. Ray had another guy in the jet with him and they couldn't or wouldn't say who was at the controls. Initially you don't think of questions to ask, that comes later. It was a while before I knew the plane had immediately caught fire and that of course was why I was told that I could not see him - that was hard to deal with. I later learned from other officers and their wives that I knew, the reason for the long delay in getting out to tell me was that [they went first to see] the other wife who lived near the station.

Later that evening Ray's mother and I think father came, also Tony. My mother and father came the next day and stayed with me until we left Red Lodge on the Thursday. During these few days someone from the RAF came a few times and a full service funeral was arranged for Friday. Tony took over all the necessary affairs that I should have done had I not been so far away. I've always thought that Tony became a mature man overnight. I wonder if I really showed my gratitude at the time.

Ray's was the first funeral I had ever attended and in truth I didn't really know what a full service funeral entailed. Maybe the fact that I was so mentally numb helped. I think it's nature's way to help keep you sane.

Lots of that day's details are blank to me - strange because I have a pretty good memory and some things are so very clear.

Once the cars turned into Whalebone Lane from the main road, they halted and an officer opened the door and helped me out. The road had been closed to other traffic and was lined each side with airmen from RAF Hornchurch. From that point on I walked behind Ray's coffin. I have no idea if Tony or Ray's Dad or anyone else walked behind me. I think I was alone. I definitely felt alone. I was determined to behave with dignity and self-control. I felt I owed it to Ray and in order to do that I was trying to close my mind off from what was really happening. I can't recall any of the service in the little church except the minister's voice saying: "In God's house there are many mansions."

Nothing else at all.

The officers from Ray's own mess were there. They carried him into the church and then to the graveside. I have distinct recollections there: the officers stood on one side and myself. I expect the other close members of the family [stood] on the other and then came the general salute, followed by buglers playing *The Last Post*. That was very difficult to cope with. The men were at the salute and I remember one of them had tears streaming down his face. I don't think I'd ever met him but that sight always remained with me.

As I've said [elsewhere] Ray's older brother Ken had been shot down in 1944. He was a Sgt Pilot posted missing, believed killed and sadly was never found. His wife Eve had a son 8 months later. She later married Jim who was great to her and her son Ian. Eve and Jim came and took Geoff and Tina to their house for that sad day.

Tina was 14 months old; Geoff 3 years 11 months. Too young I felt to understand anything about what was happening, especially as this was not a simple funeral. It would have been pretty frightening. The gunfire alone would have been scary for them [although Geoff has said quite recently that he wishes he had attended his Dad's funeral]. The day finally quietened down and I had my children back. That helped me. My children seemed the only people that were real, small as they were.

[Later entry, undated]

Tony and Jean did come on that first evening to Red Lodge apparently. I said that my recollections were poor about what did happen. Tony tells me that he walked beside me [behind the coffin] and Jean was able to say that 250 Airmen lined the road. She asked if I remembered throwing the clock. I had no idea, but apparently I threw it really hard across the bedroom when it went off. I can only imagine that it had been set the previous day to wake Ray (I know he left early). I threw it in frustration, I suppose but I can recall nothing about that and it sounds so unlike me.

After the funeral I stayed with Ray's mother and father until I found a house to live in. Geoff's birthday – 12th December – came quickly and I remember making him a special cake, shaped like a railway engine with a Swiss roll for the main boiler and a square piece of chocolate cake for where the coal was fed in. I know Smarties got me out of trouble for buffers etc. and chocolate mints for wheels. Then came Christmas and I was determined to find Geoff a really nice bike – and I did.

****

I have no memory of my father, just photographs and stories: pictures of an impossibly handsome young man in uniform and the idealised stories of those who die before their time. When I was a seven-year-old child at boarding school, the stories sustained me in my loneliness. They served me well; they helped me survive. As a young man, I unconsciously sought to emulate him when I joined the police service (another uniformed organisation) and worked my way up the ranks, thinking occasionally that he might have been proud of what I had achieved. Increasingly as the years passed and the apparently secure frameworks of marriage, family and career began to totter, I yearned for him.

In my forties I joined a men's group that met periodically in Roeburndale, Lancashire. On 18th June 1995, which happened to be Father's Day, I was in for a surprise. Late in the afternoon I went for a solitary walk and lay down to look through the wooden slats of a rickety footbridge suspended over a river. It was bright sunshine, though it had rained heavily the night before, and the sunlight glittered on the swollen blood-red torrent as it rushed beneath me.

I was mesmerised by the scintillating light half-blinding my eyes and the sound of the water filling my ears with what sounded like a wild song.

Forgetting that I was supposed to be a sensible grown-up man, I sang back to the river in hoarse high-pitched tones that were snatched away by the rushing water. This strange and unexpected musical conversation seemed to expand my consciousness. Roeburndale was an ancient, unspoiled valley and I was willing to believe it still had magic. My rational mind relaxed its grip and I felt completely present and wide open to everything around me.

In that moment I noticed a charred tree-stump caught on a rock, swaying in the current. And in some extraordinary fashion that I can neither explain nor describe, though it did not change shape, it became my father's body. My heart pounding, I stumbled into the water and dragged him ashore. I could feel his presence so strongly that I sat on the bank with my arms around the tree-stump and I – the man who had forgotten how to cry – cried like the child I had been when he died. I could imagine that the river was weeping too, his tears perhaps. In that way, we cried together for what we had both lost when he died. We cried and we laughed at the impossible joy of being together again.

"I have missed you so much," I said aloud.

"You are my son. I love you," was his wordless reply.

We stayed together by the riverbank until dusk and then I carried the tree-stump up the steep side of the valley and placed it on a boulder so that he could keep guard over me sleeping down below at the campsite. That night I slept a sweet, dreamless sleep as though resting like a child in his arms without any care or burden.

The next morning I told the other men about my experience and led them up through the long, wet grass to the tree-stump perched on the boulder. As we arrived at the boulder, a solitary fighter jet passed high overhead in the sky above like a sign saying, "I am here". I wept again for my father, this time as a man surrounded by other men, feeling the strength of their arms as they held me up, seeing their own tears falling and mingling with mine on the ground – a libation for all our fathers.

I sensed that he had come to say goodbye, had come for me to return him to the friendly earth and mourn him as I had been unable to do as a child. It was time to let go of a ghost so that I could have a real father – one who had lived well and died early. As I sat on the boulder beside my father's image, some of the other men dug a grave in a small wild garden by the river. When they returned, we carried the tree-stump in a funeral procession and placed it in the ground. Together, we covered it with soil and smoothed the earth down as if tucking him in bed under a green quilt. Then someone asked if I wanted to say anything. I thought for a moment and the words came easily:

"My father could fly – and it cost him his life. He was a strong man, a loving man, and fearless. If he had been different, he might have lived longer, but he died doing what he loved best and I am proud of him. His name was Raymond Geoffrey Mead and he died in 1953, aged twenty-eight years. Thank you for helping me to bury him today. Goodbye Dad – I love you – Rest in Peace."

*****

I knew you by your absence,
like leaves moving in the wind
or footprints in the snow.

You left a space I couldn't fill,
an ocean unmoved by longing,
indifferent to my tears.

So I shut you away inside myself;
I slammed and locked the door
and long since lost the key.

It took me years to understand
it wasn't you I had imprisoned
behind that steel door, but me.

You cut a swathe across the sky
to teach me what you knew:
Only love can set you free.

*****